Coloring Pages For Kids Dogs Coloring Book

Coloring Books for Kids

By Gala Publication

Published by:

Gala Publication

ISBN-13: 978- 1508659457
ISBN-10: 1508659451

©Copyright 2015 – Gala Publication

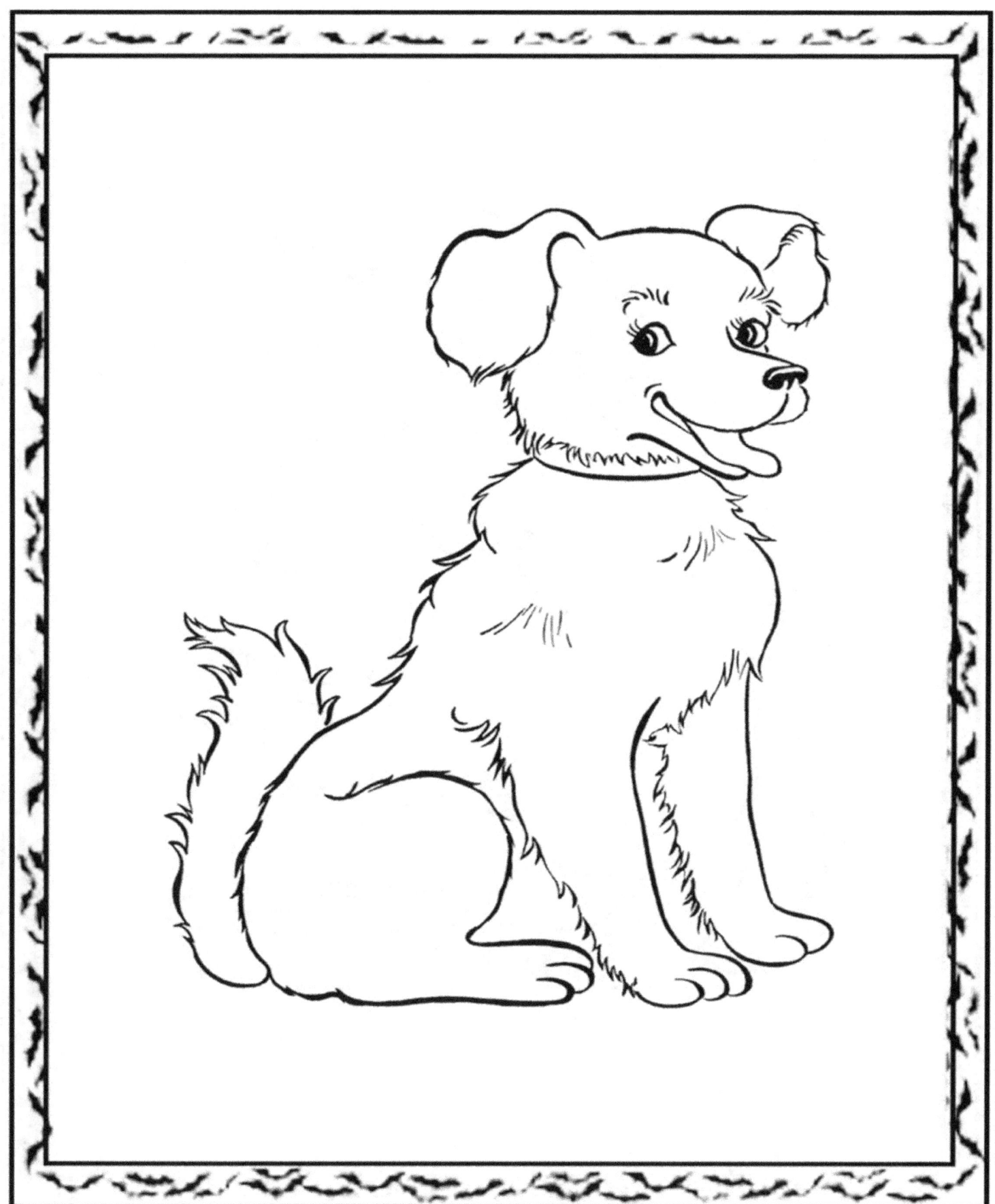

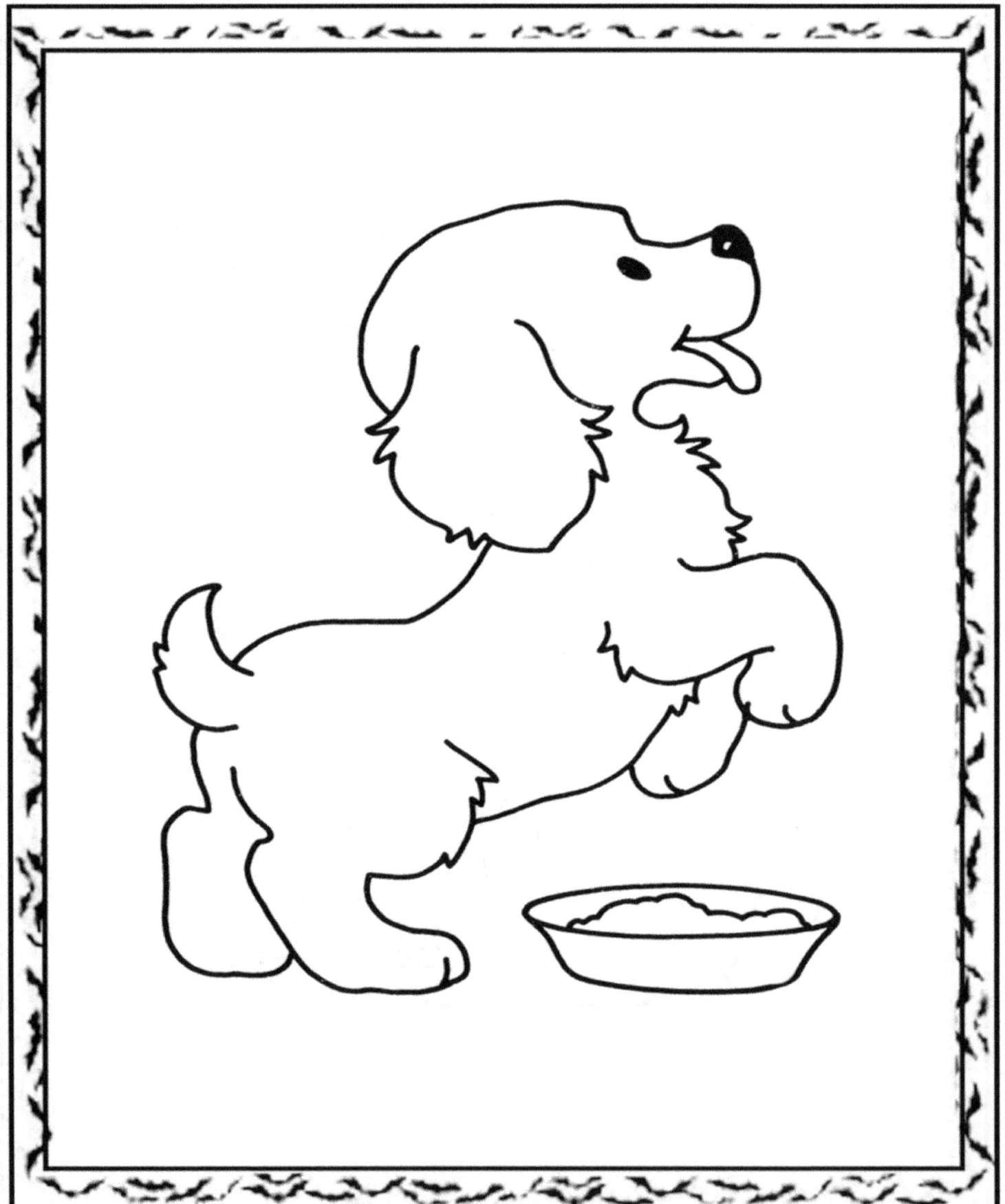

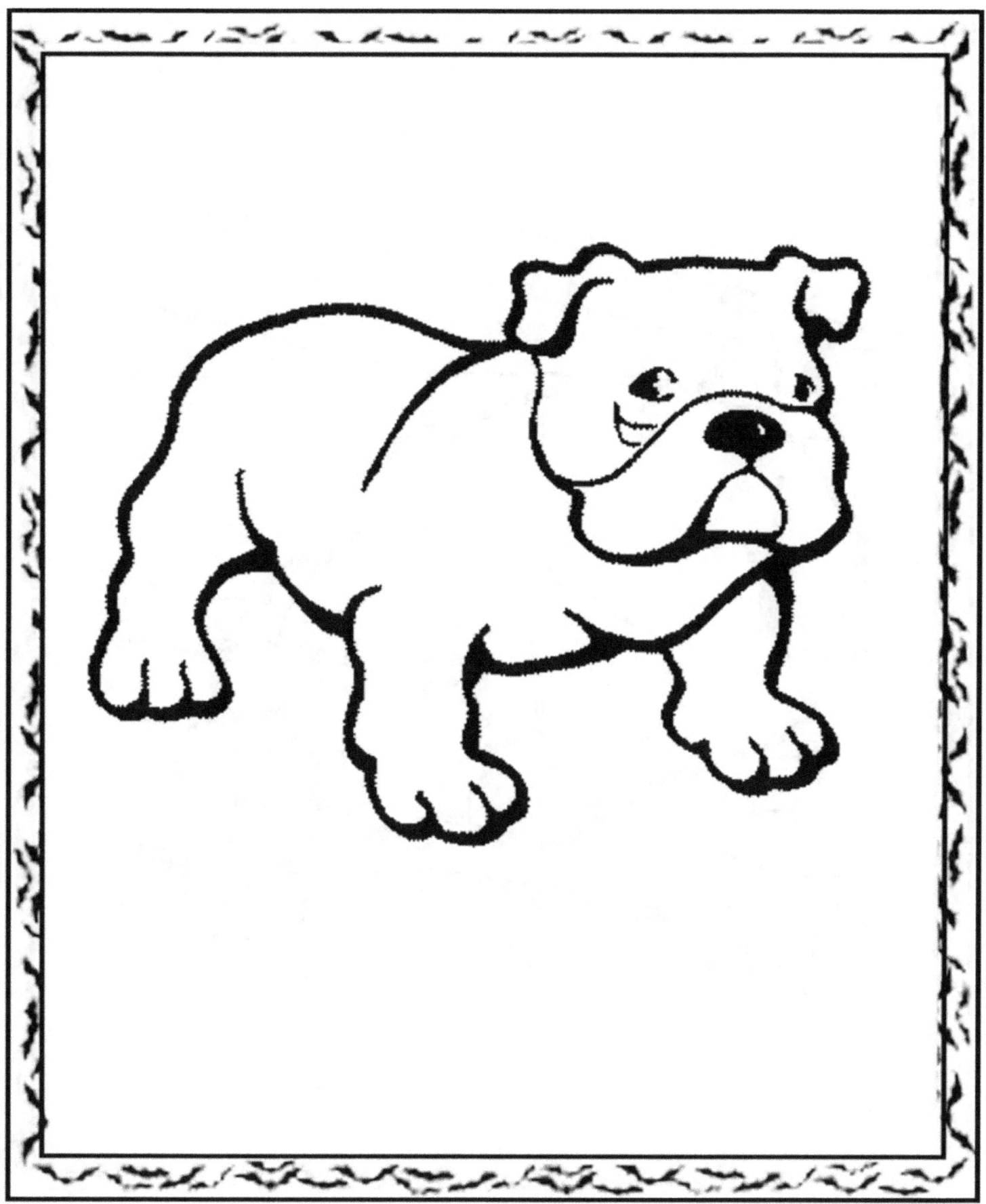

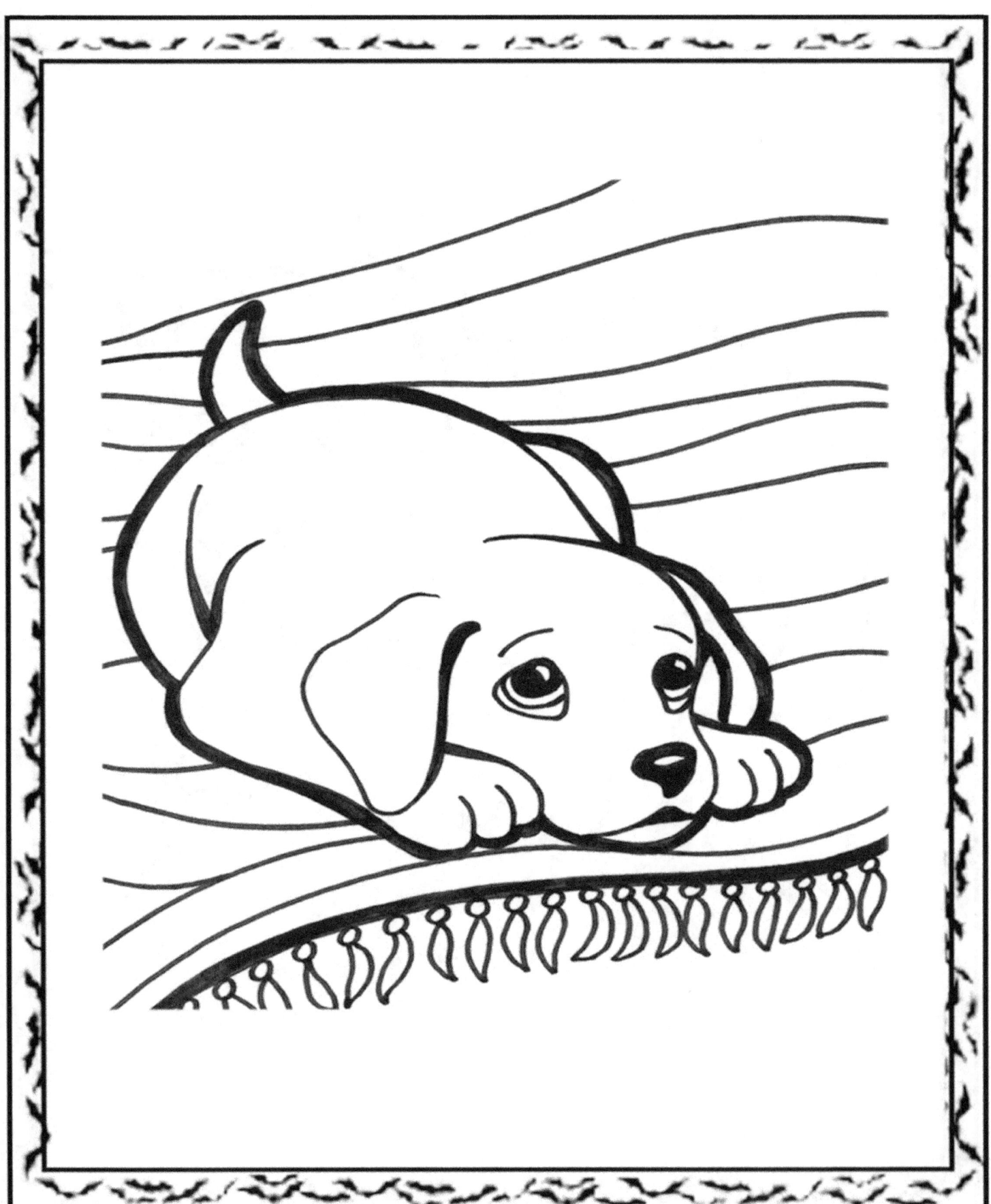

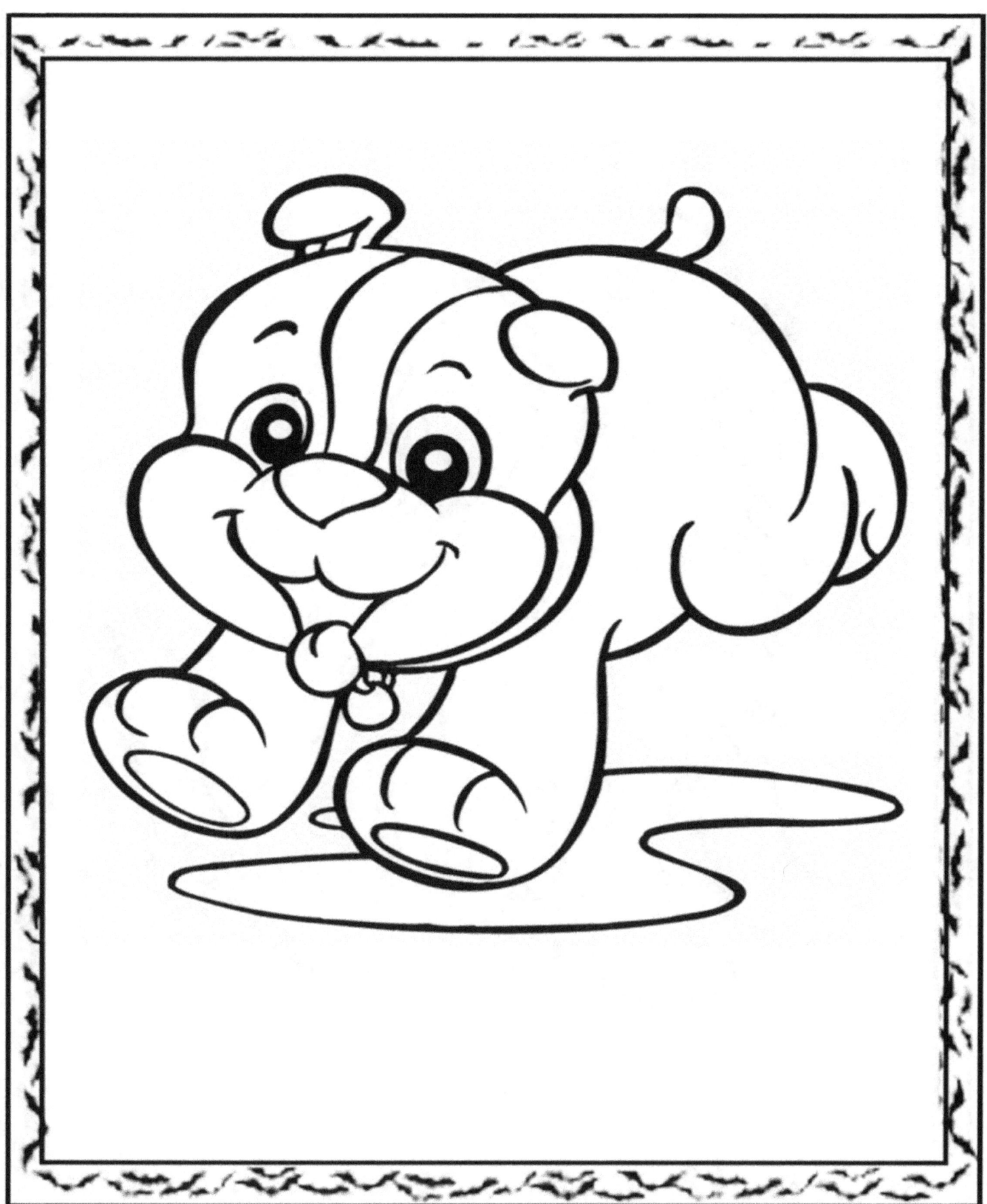

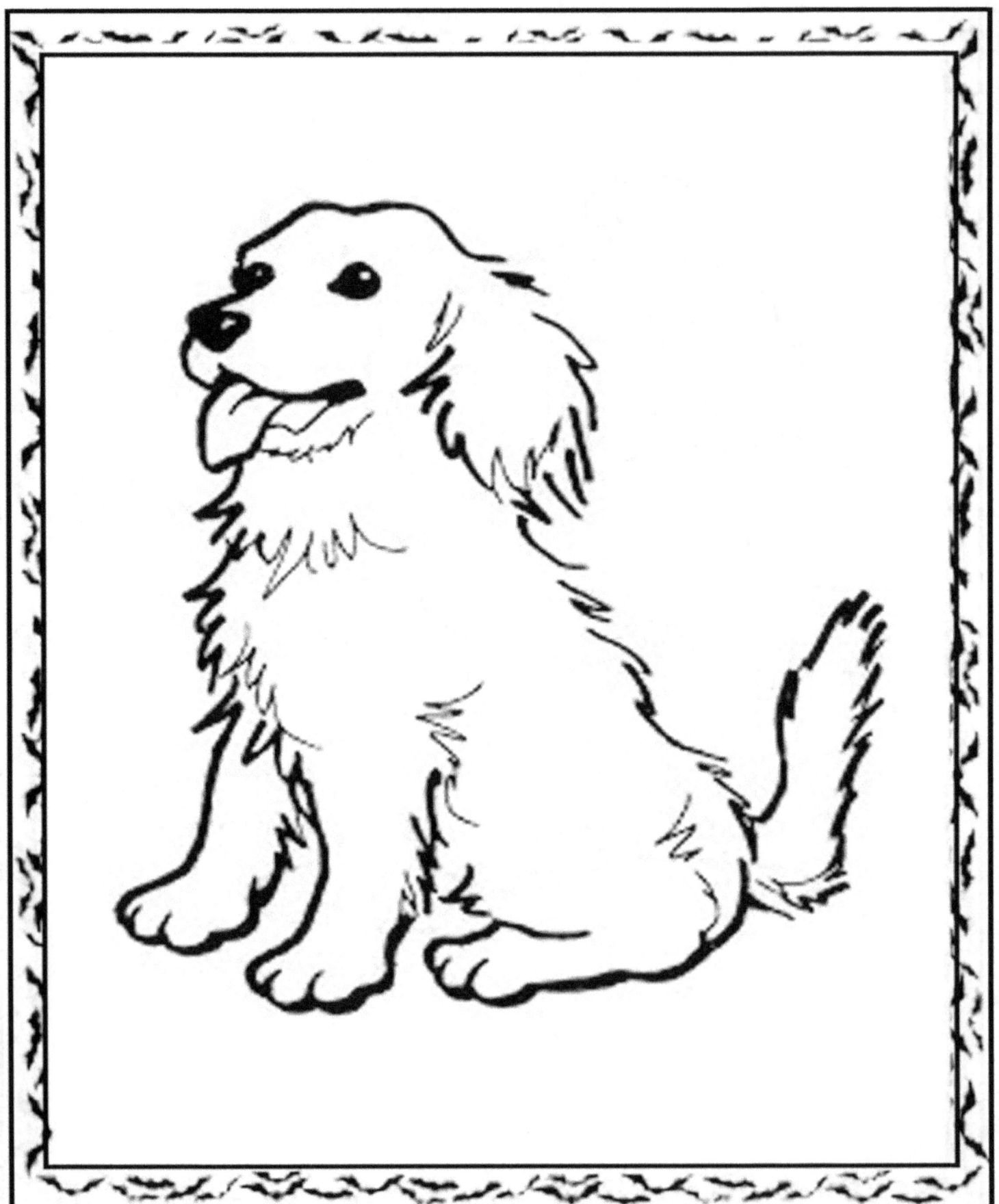

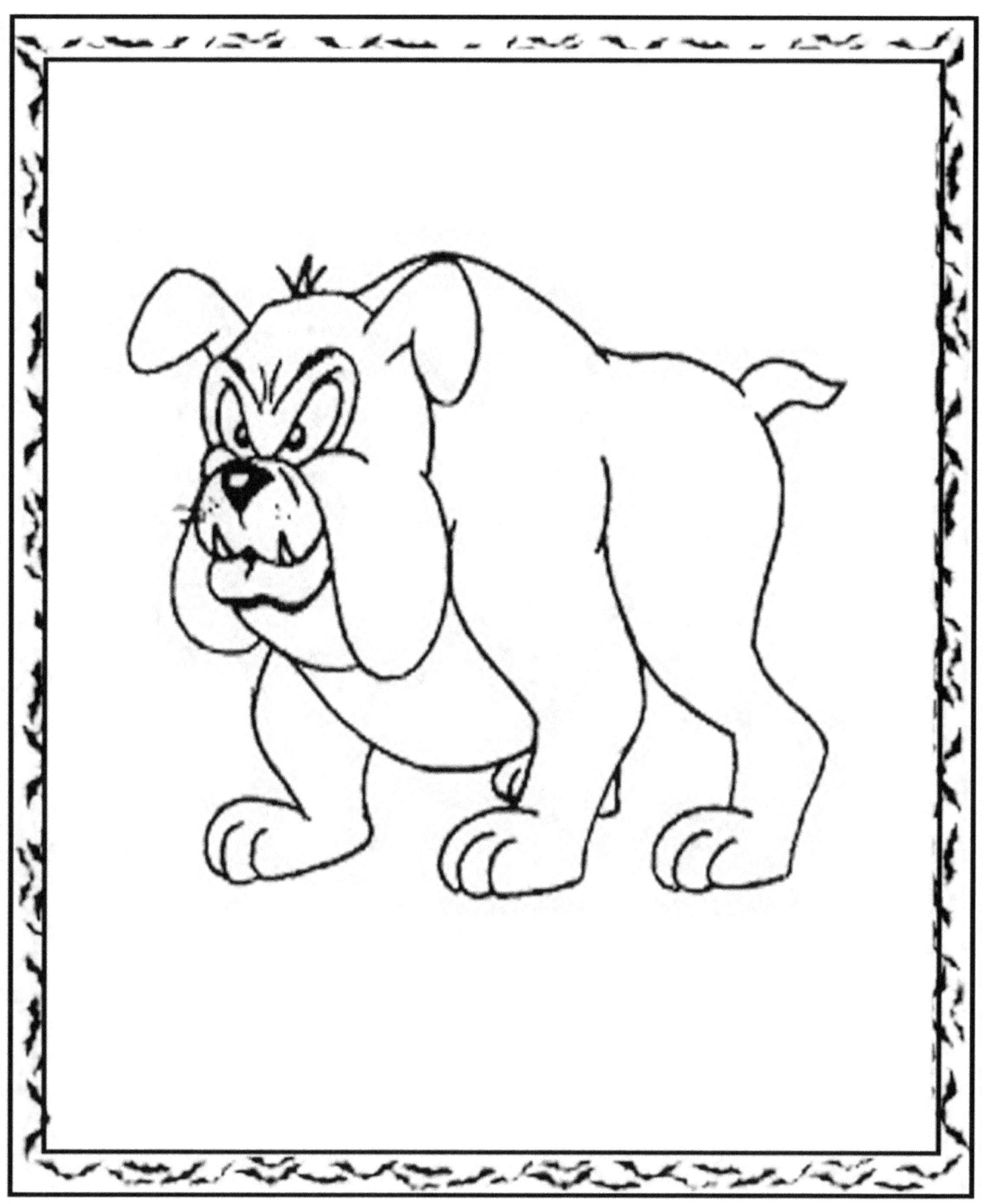

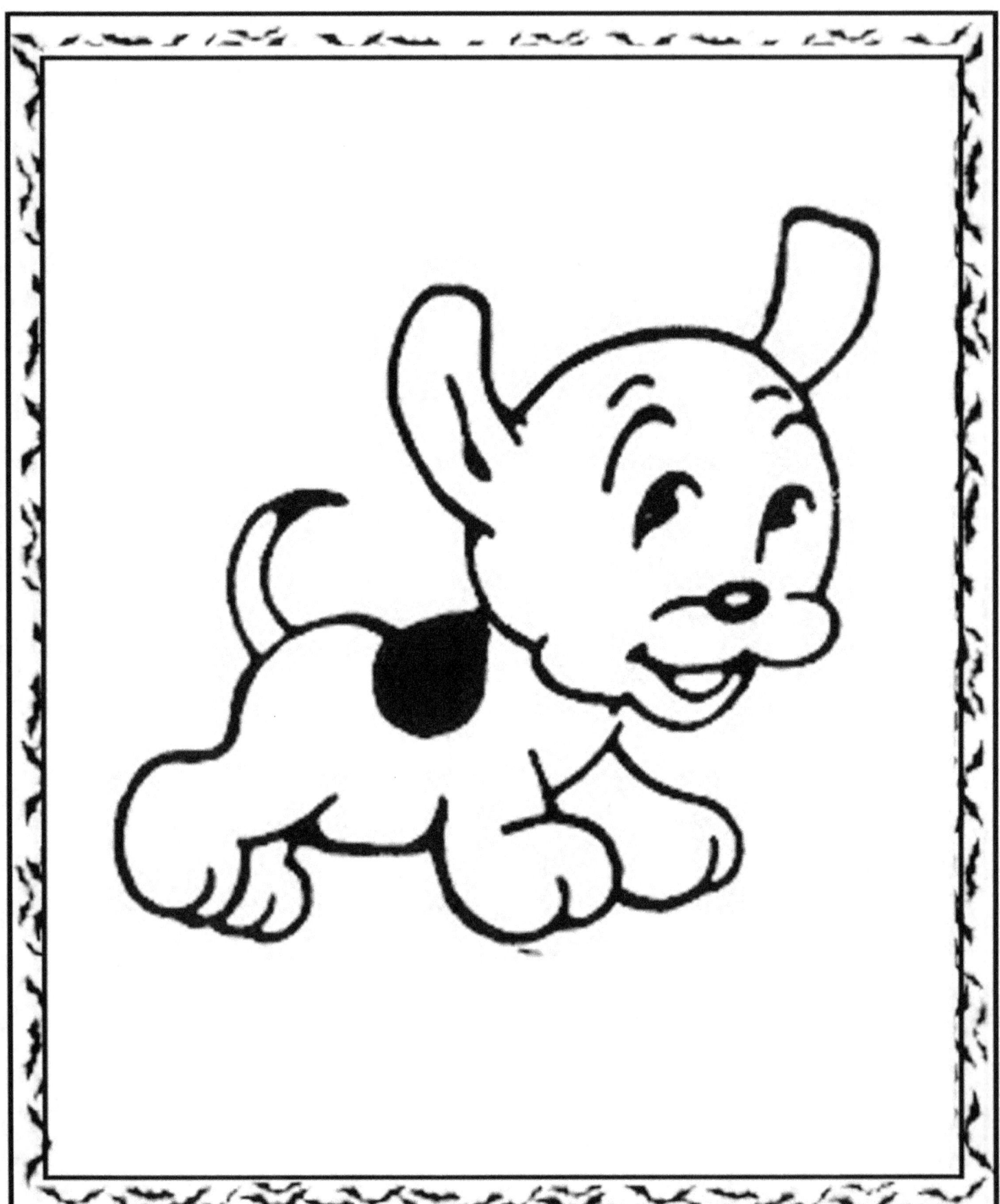

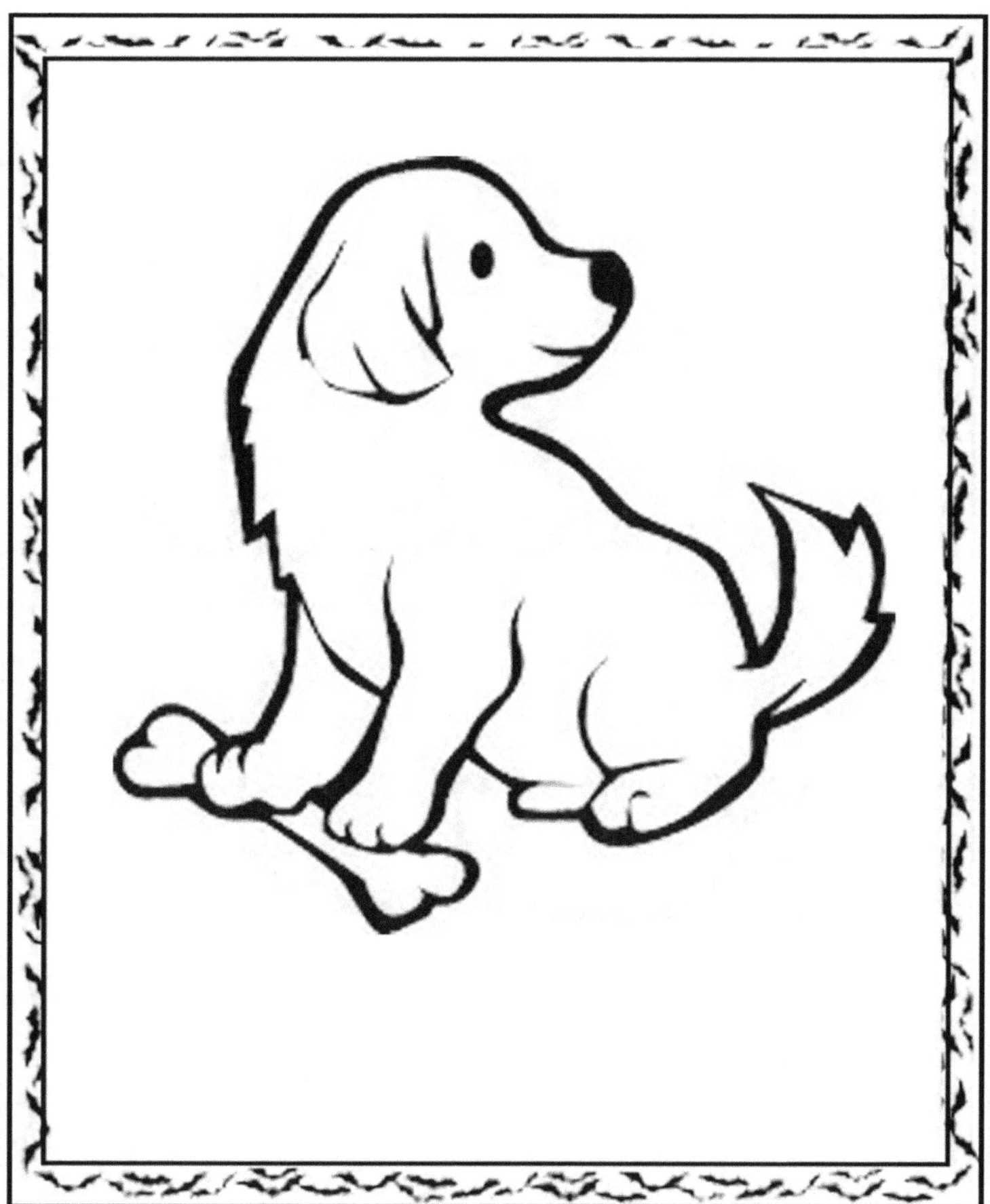

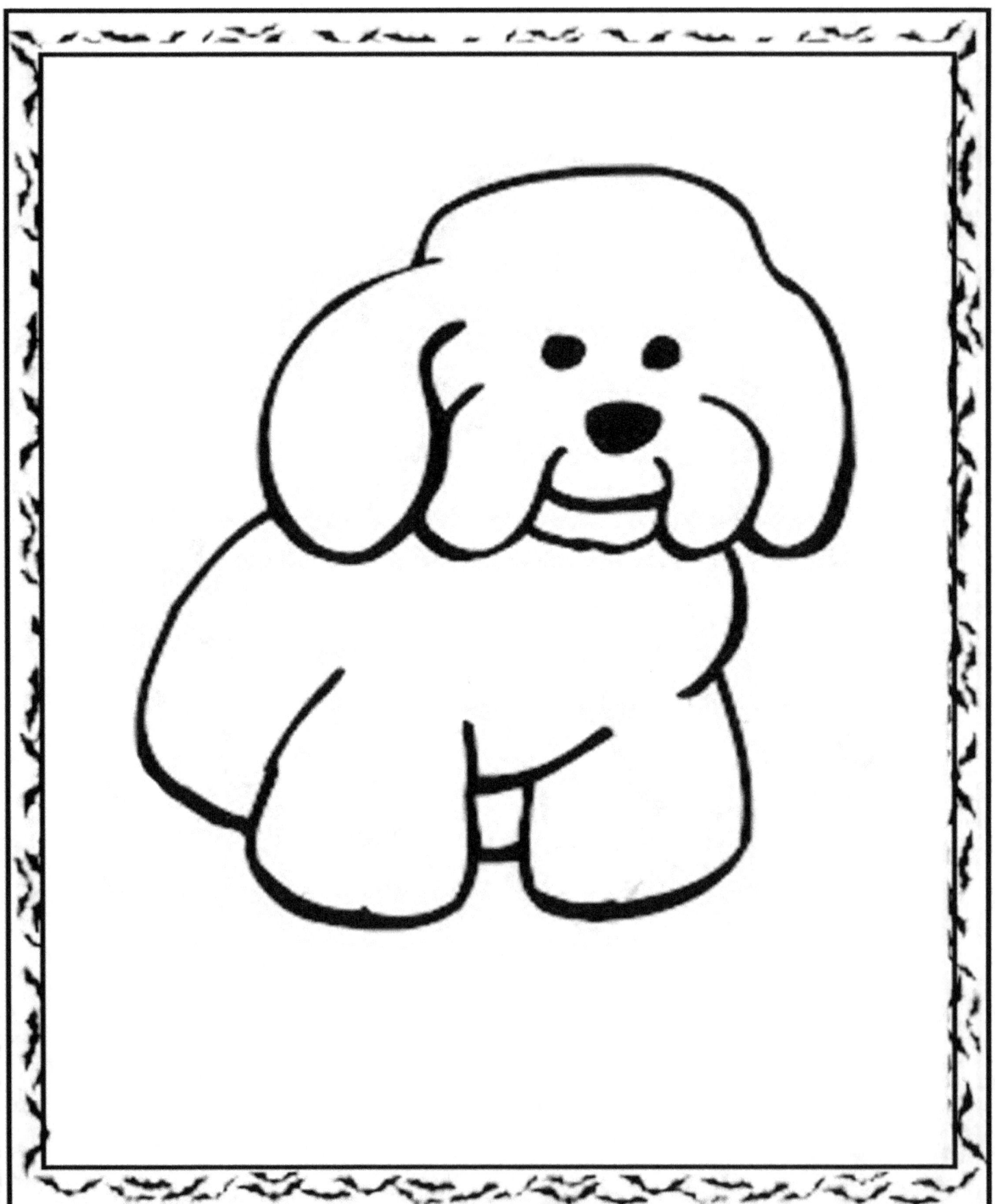

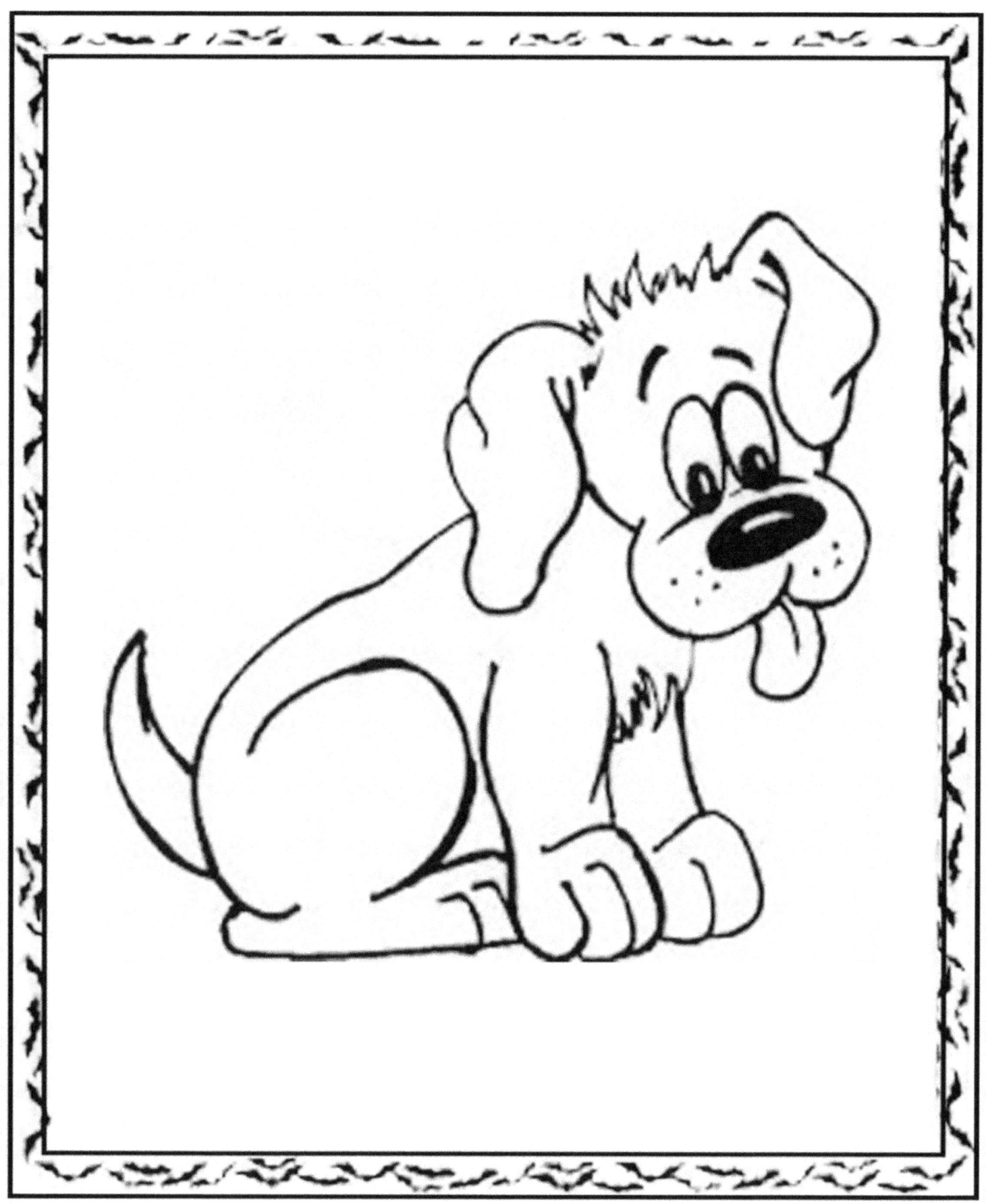

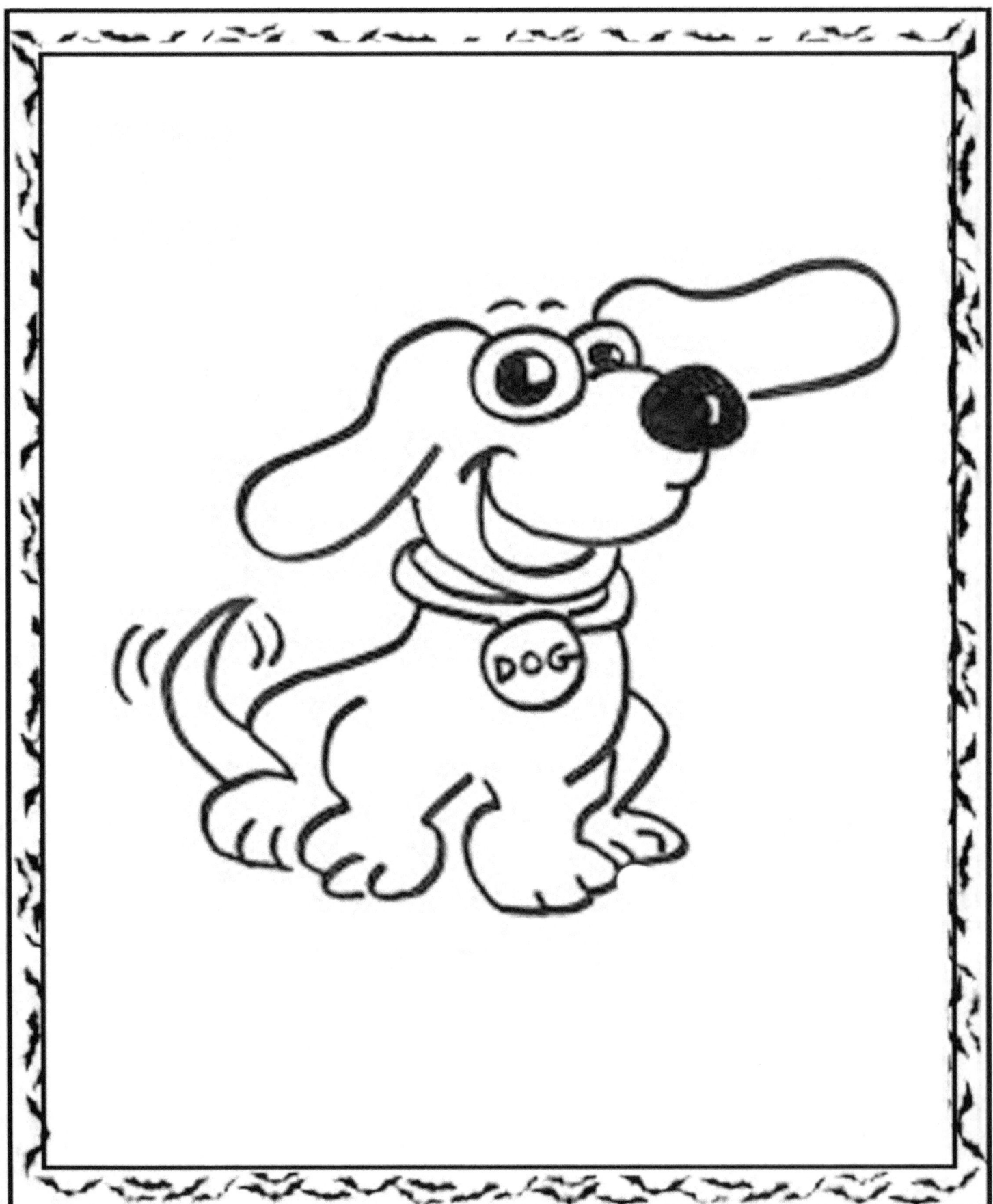

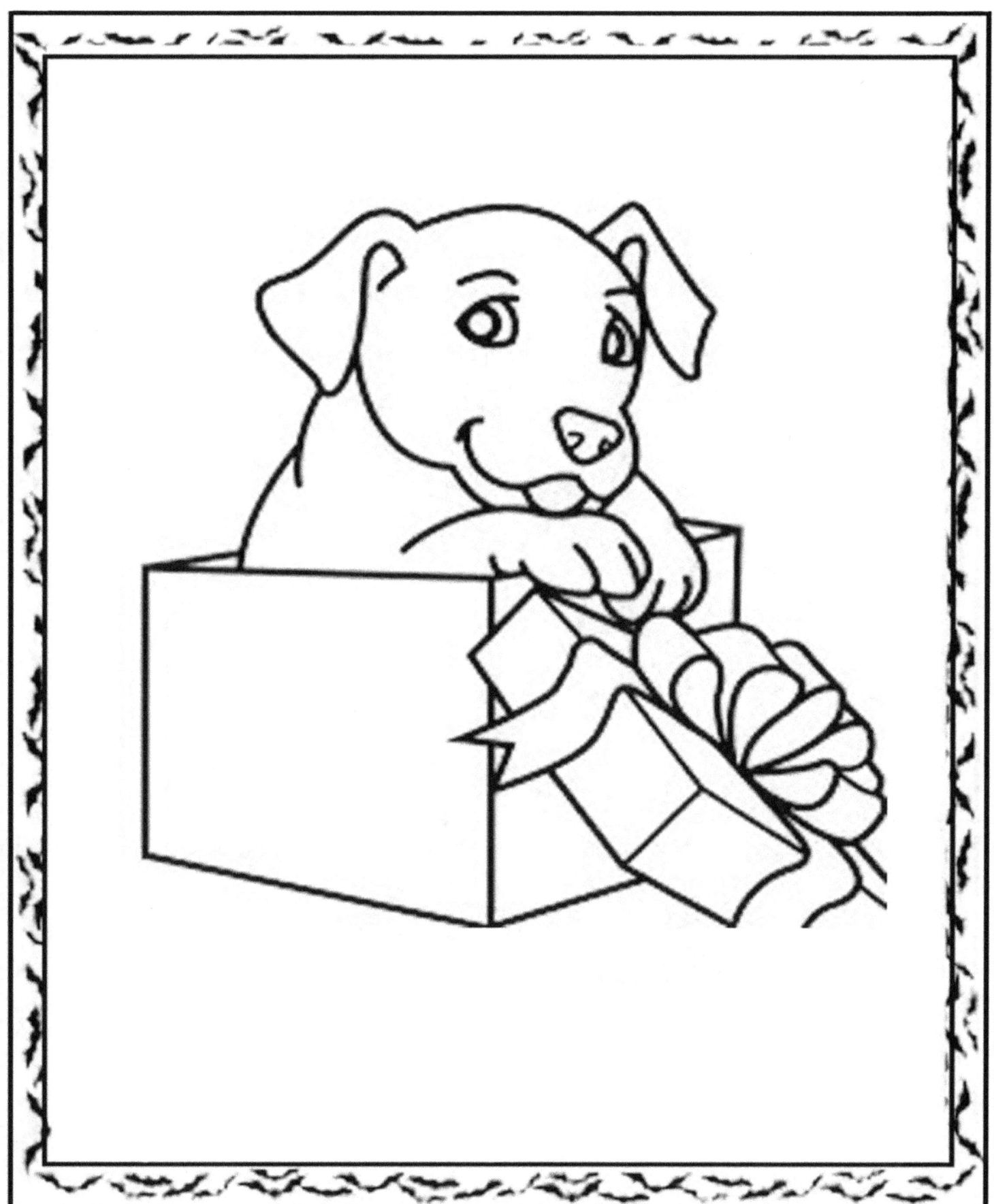

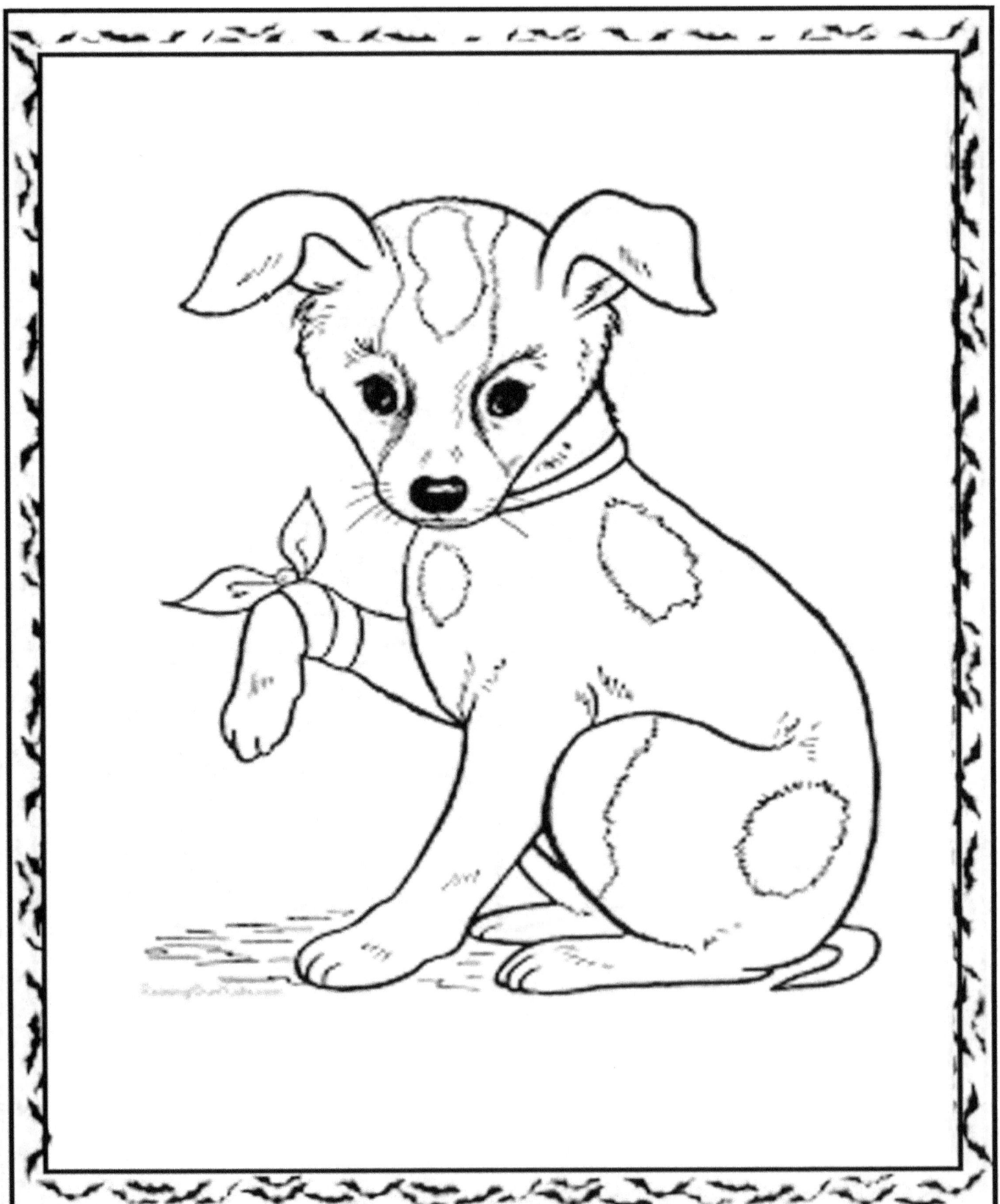

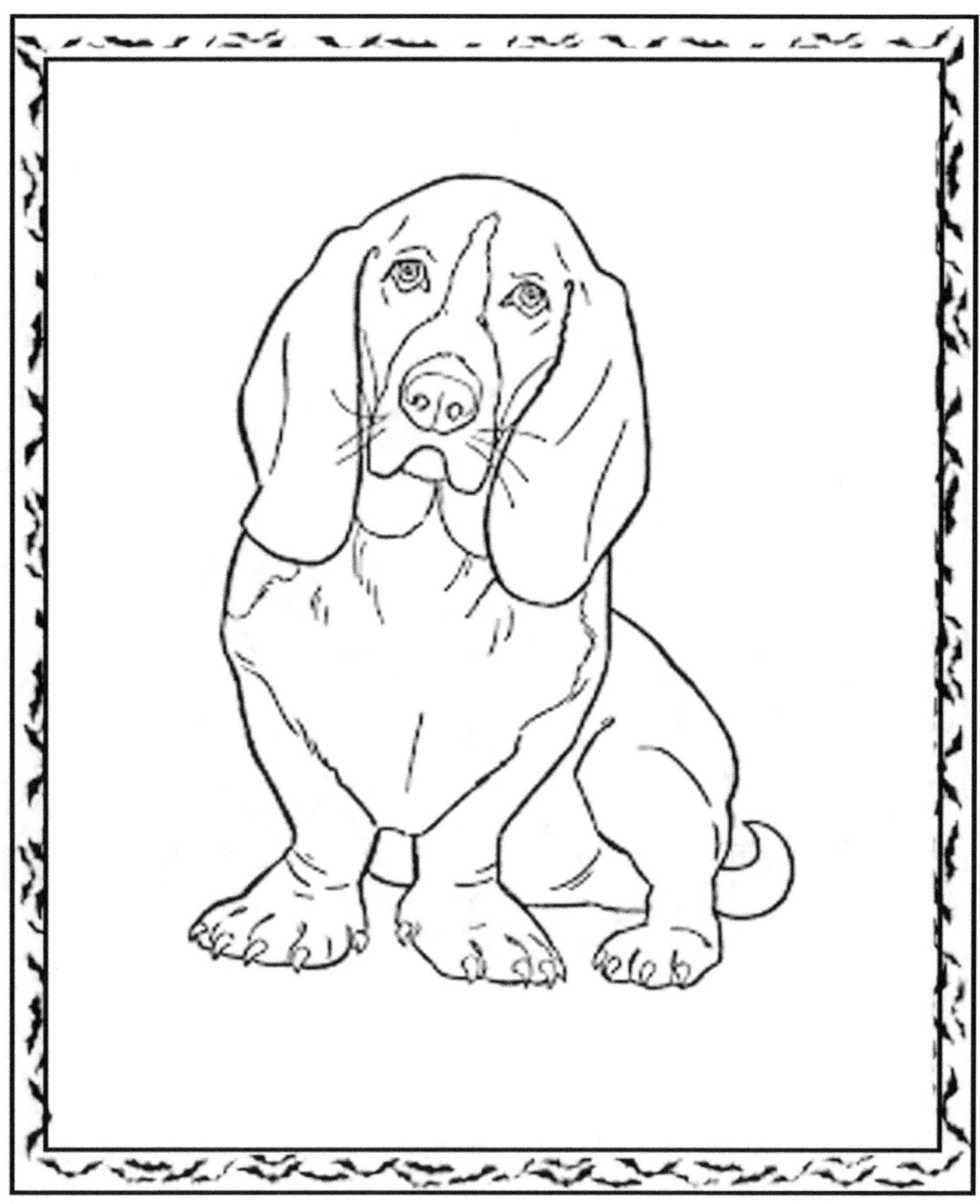

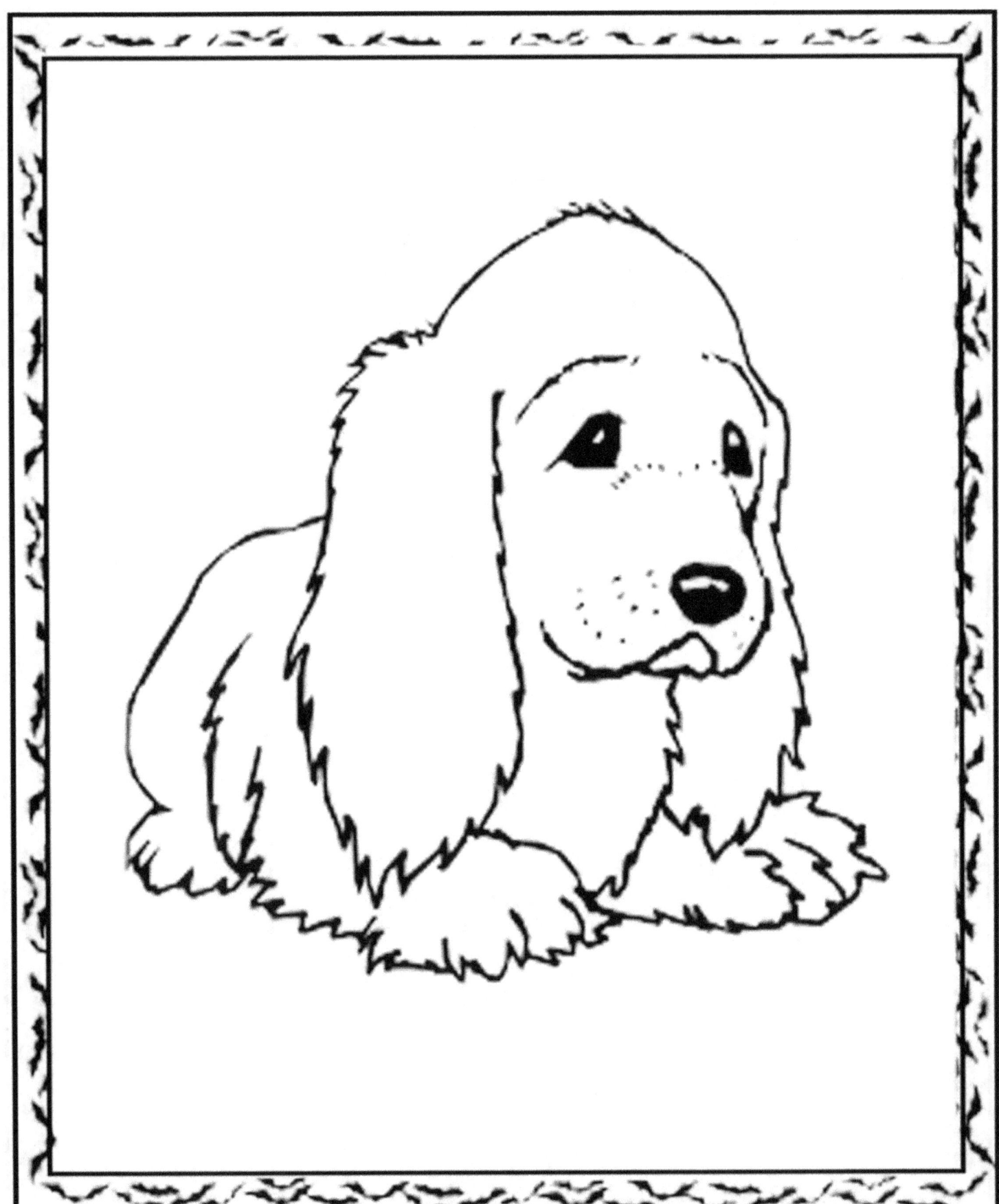

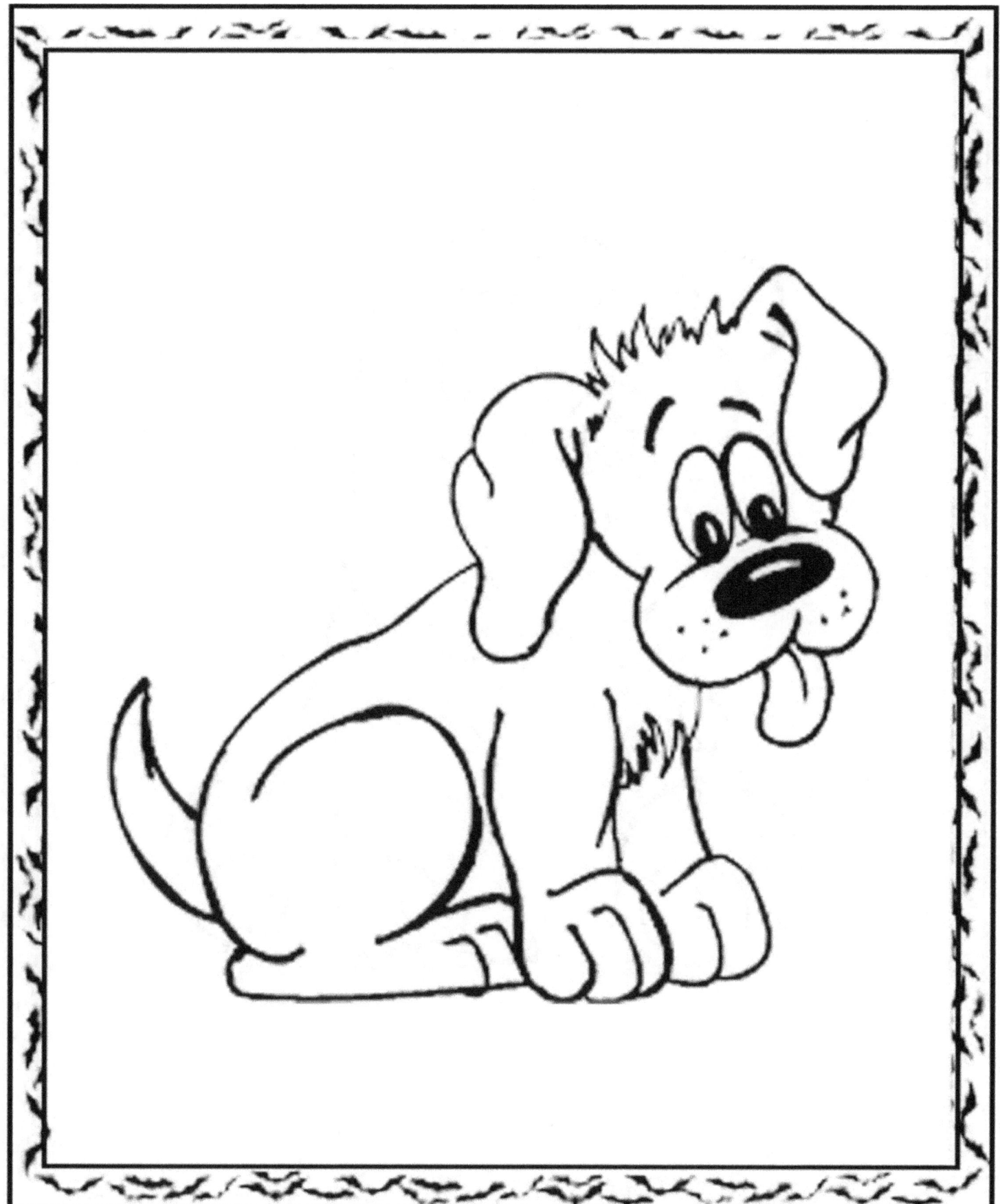

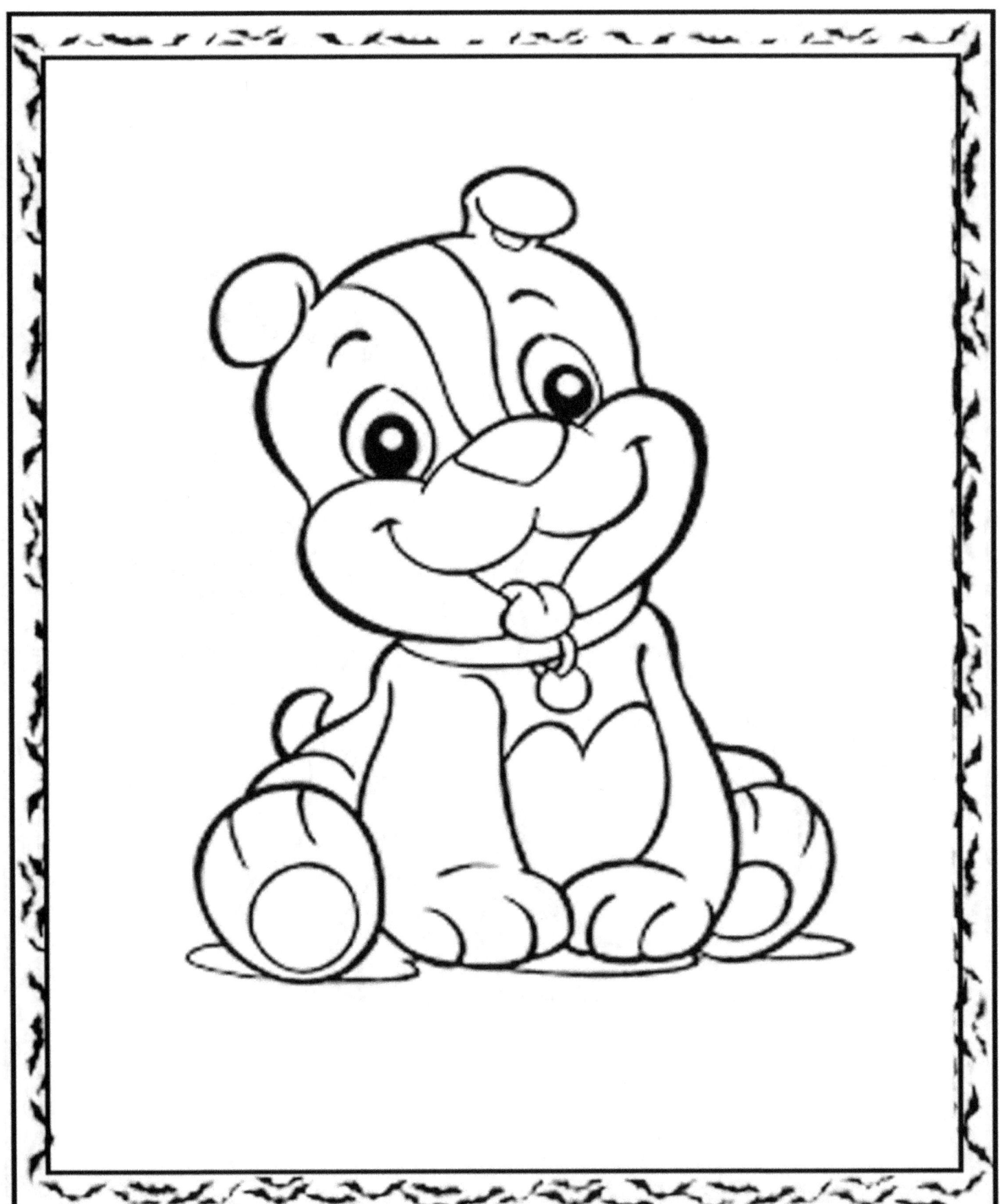

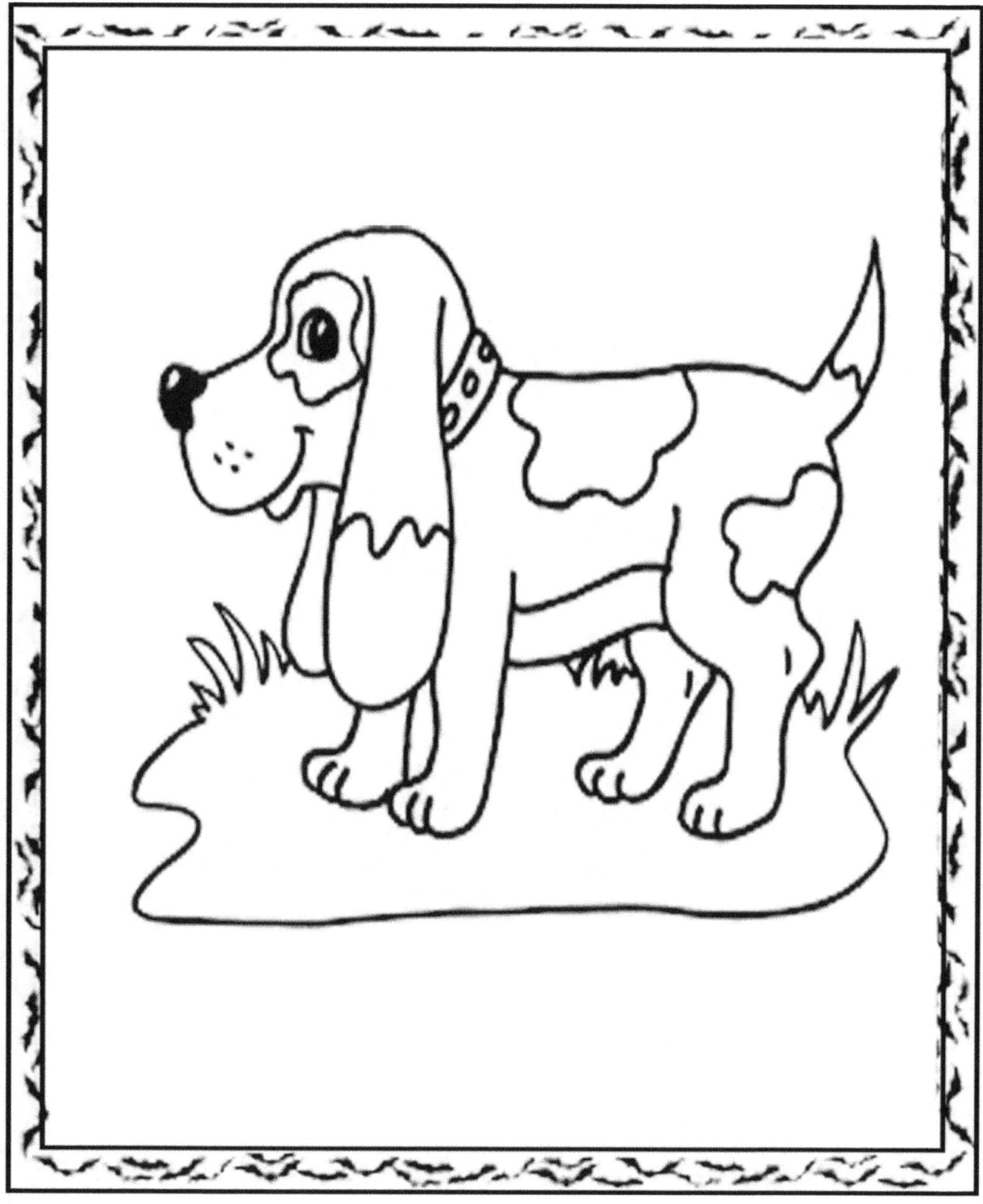

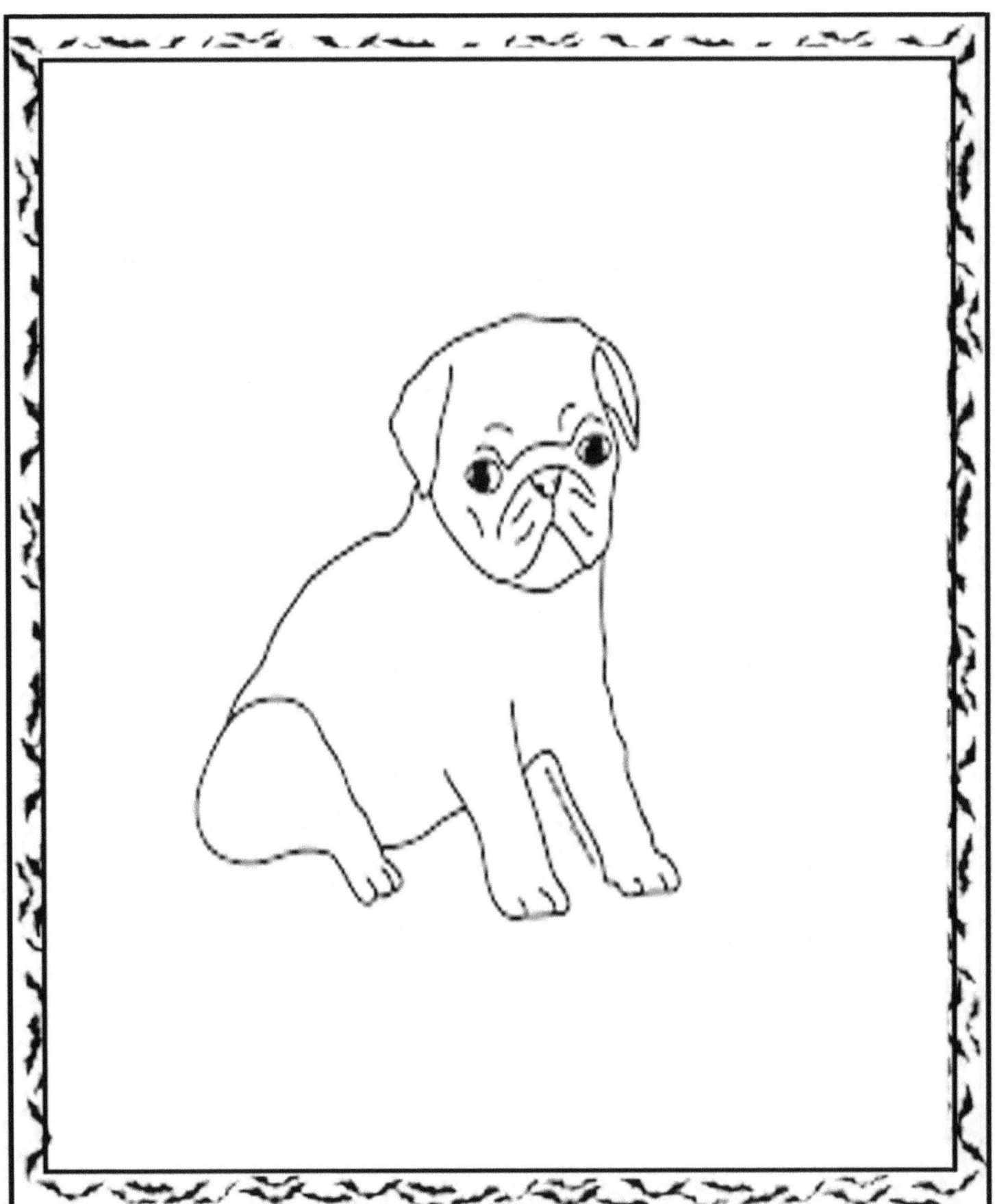

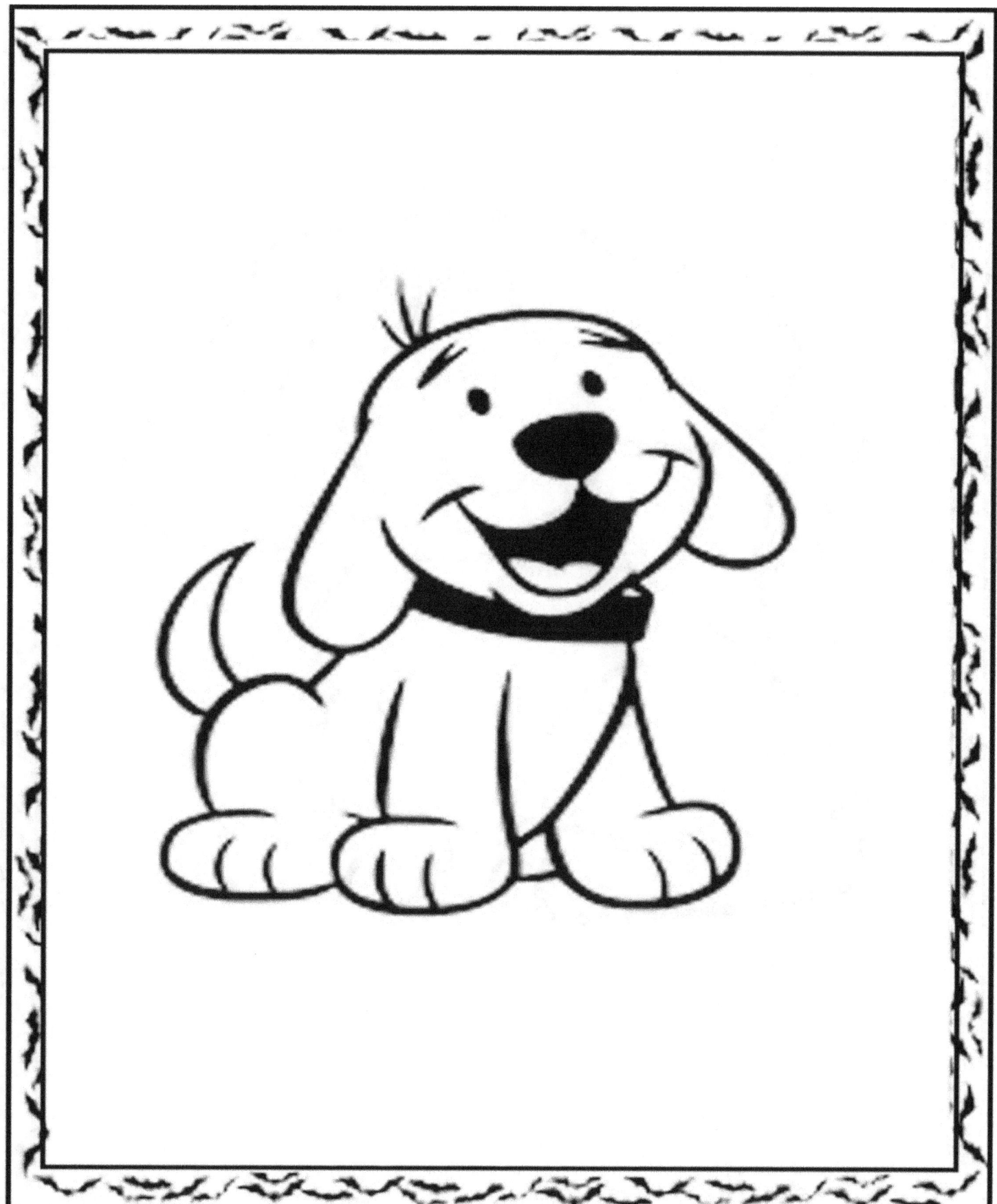

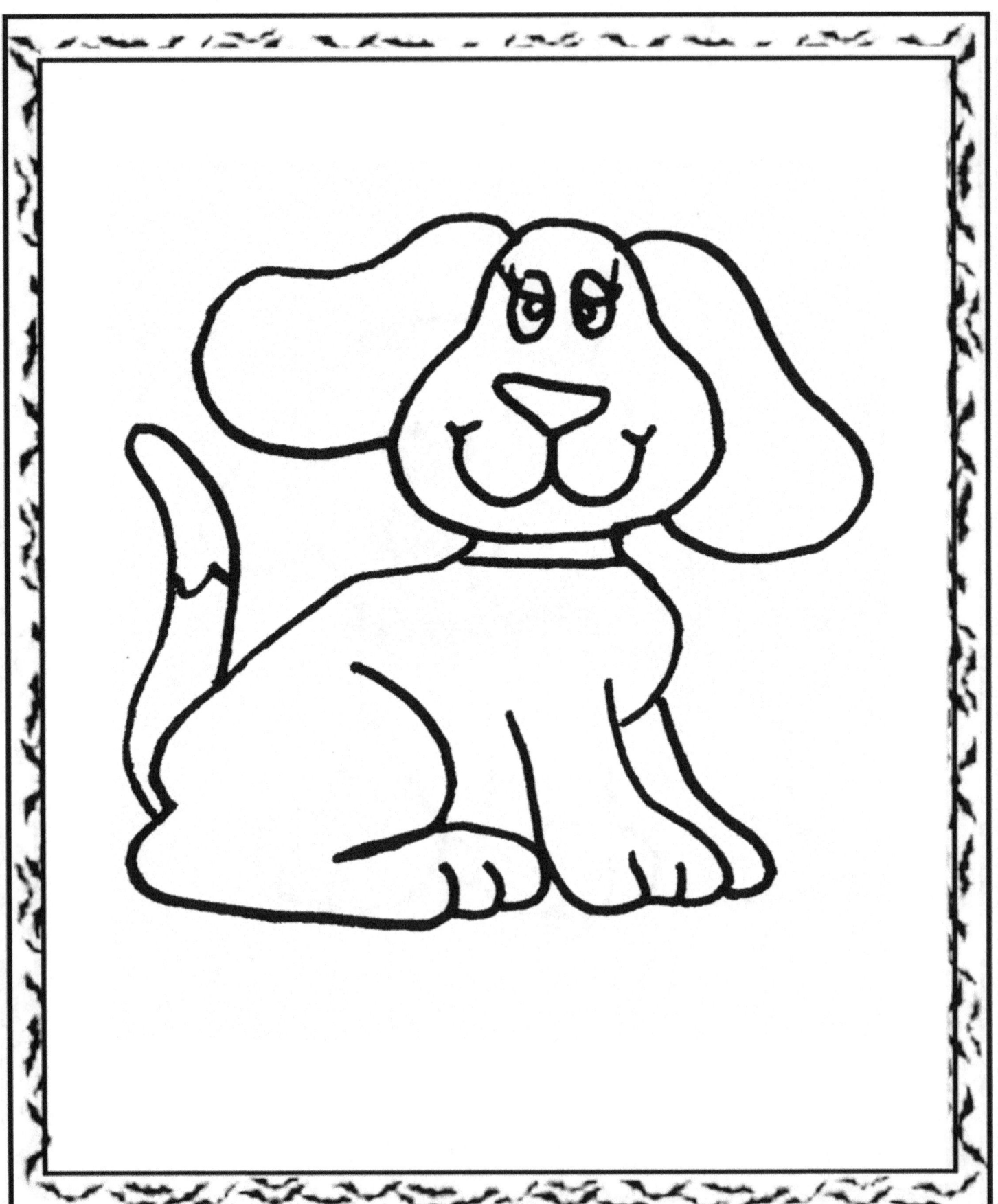

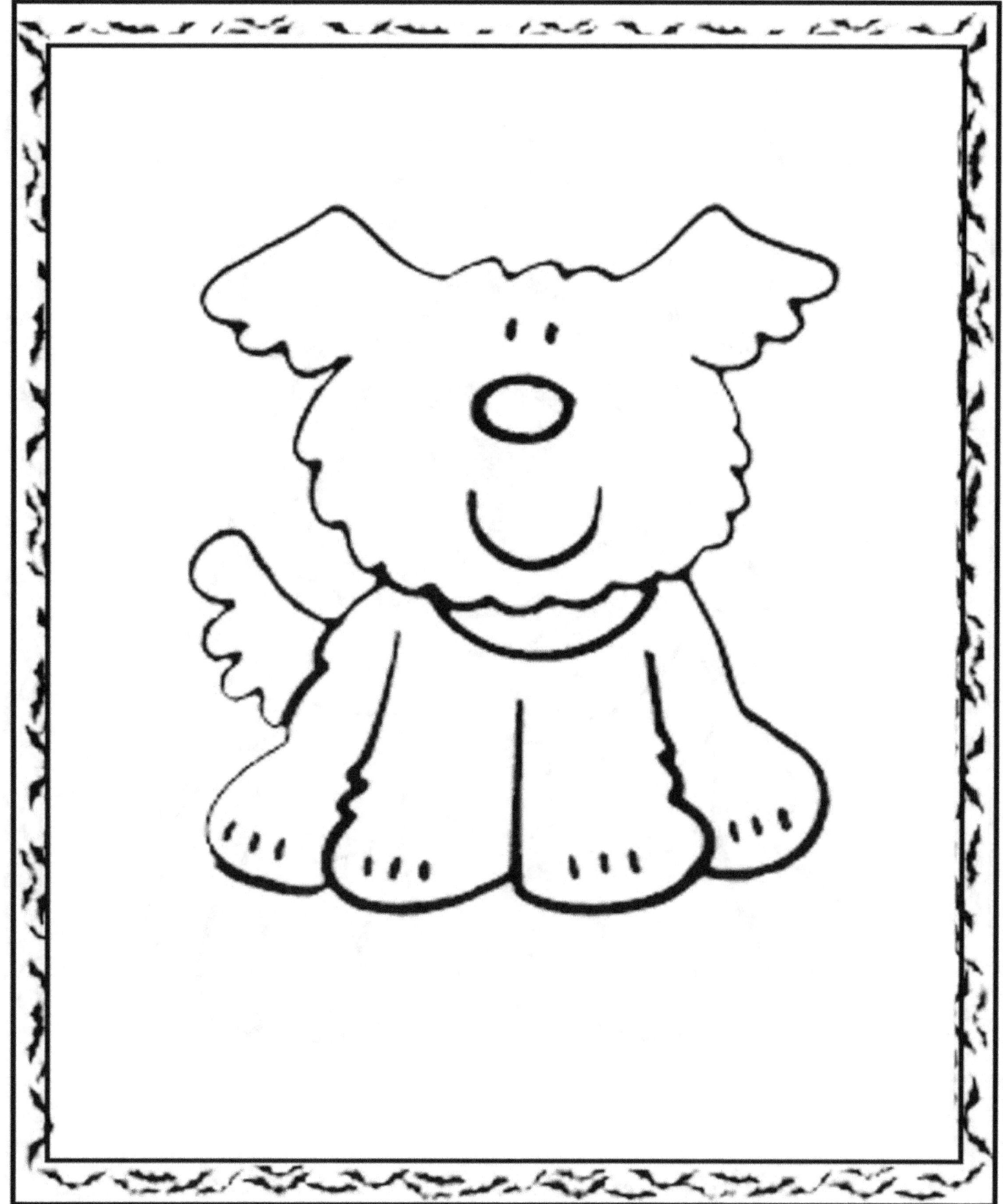

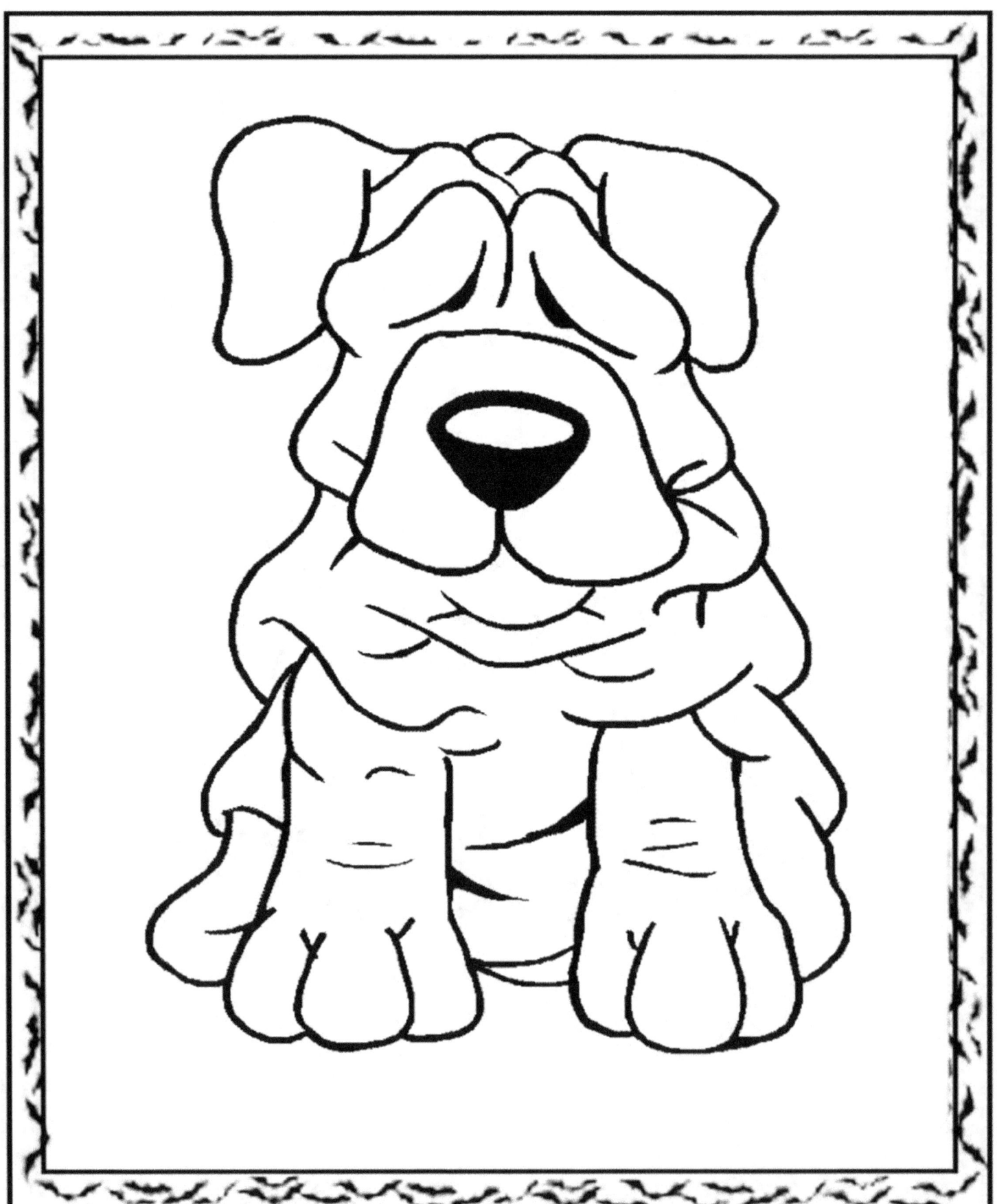

THE END